EMERGENCY RESPONSE

POLICE

PROTECT AND SERVE

Tom Greve

Rourke
Educational Media
rourkeeducationalmedia.com

Scan for Related Titles and
Teacher Resources

Before Reading:

Building Academic Vocabulary and Background Knowledge

Before reading a book, it is important to tap into what your child or students already know about the topic. This will help them develop their vocabulary, increase their reading comprehension, and make connections across the curriculum.

1. Look at the cover of the book. What will this book be about?
2. What do you already know about the topic?
3. Let's study the Table of Contents. What will you learn about in the book's chapters?
4. What would you like to learn about this topic? Do you think you might learn about it from this book? Why or why not?
5. Use a reading journal to write about your knowledge of this topic. Record what you already know about the topic and what you hope to learn about the topic.
6. Read the book.
7. In your reading journal, record what you learned about the topic and your response to the book.
8. After reading the book complete the activities below.

Content Area Vocabulary
Read the list. What do these words mean?

analytics
appoints
bribes
brutality
capitol
details
elected
emergencies
fiction
interstate
municipal
population
rural
society
suburban
sworn
taxes
undercover
urban

After Reading:

Comprehension and Extension Activity

After reading the book, work on the following questions with your child or students in order to check their level of reading comprehension and content mastery.

1. How do the duties of urban police officers differ from those of rural police officers? (Summarize)
2. How has technology changed police work? (Asking questions)
3. What was the first paid police force in the U.S. called? (Summarize)
4. What tools does an officer need? (Summarize)
5. Hollywood has made police work seem glamorous. How can this perception effect kids who want to become police officers? (Infer)

Extension Activity

Show what you know! Draw a police officer and label all the important tools the officer needs each day. Then write 5 facts about police officers. Share this information with a partner.

TABLE OF CONTENTS

It's evening in the supermarket. A boy and his friends wait in line to pay for their snacks. Suddenly, the crash of colliding shopping carts and angry shouting pierces the normal sound of the store.

The boys look toward the noise of the scuffle. They see a person running out of the store. He's followed by the store's owner, who is shouting.

"Hey! Come back here! I'm calling the police!"

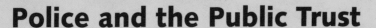

Police and the Public Trust

The public depends on the police to fight and investigate crimes, and to protect the public from criminal harm and other kinds of **emergencies**. Police carry the public trust in their **sworn** duties as officers of the law. This trust helps maintain peace in modern **society**.

Like firefighters rushing toward deadly danger, police have to be ready to respond to dangerous situations at a moment's notice.

JUSTICE FOR ALL

POLICE

Police serve, along with firefighters, paramedics, and emergency medical technicians, as first responders. When there is an emergency, they rush to the scene to help people in danger.

Police have the duty to uphold and enforce the laws of the town, district, state, or even the country in which they work. They are public employees. Their pay comes from money collected in **taxes**.

In the United States, police represent the first part of the three-tiered criminal justice system. The three parts of the criminal justice system work together to discover truth and carry out justice. The courts carry special powers to judge police and corrections officers if their members stand accused of a crime while performing their jobs.

CRIMINAL JUSTICE SYSTEM

Police
- Enforce laws
- Investigate crimes

Courts
- Allow for trials for accused
- Judge, jury, attorneys

Corrections Officers
- Operate prisons

Police arrest people who they believe have broken the law. In court, they are judged as guilty or not guilty of the crime. If they are convicted of a crime, the corrections department may put them in prison.

Police officers take an oath of service when they join a department. This is why police are sworn officers of the law. Most sworn police officers in the U.S. work for **municipal** police departments.

Nearly every state has its own police force. Often called state troopers, the state police patrol the nation's **interstate** highway systems. They also guard state **capitol** buildings.

EMERGENCY FACT
Out of 50 states, 49 have state troopers. Only Hawaii does not.

U.S. Police Officers: By The Numbers

there are more than **900,000 POLICE OFFICERS** working in more than **17,000** municipal, state, and federal **POLICE** departments

there are about **315,000,000** people in the U.S., meaning there is roughly **ONE** police officer for every **350 PEOPLE**

ABOUT 11% of **ALL OFFICERS** are **FEMALE**

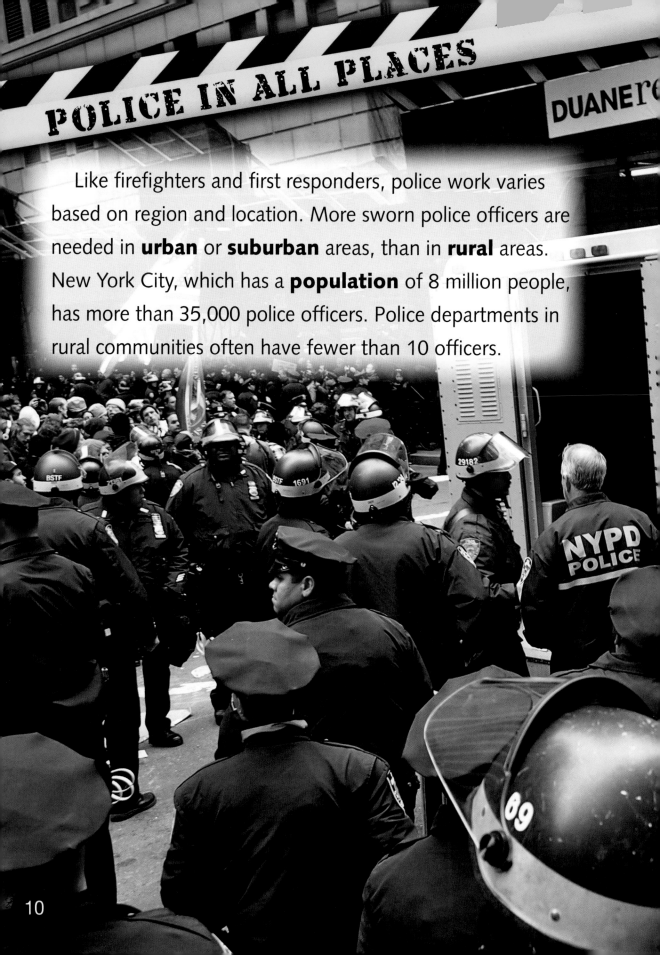

Like firefighters and first responders, police work varies based on region and location. More sworn police officers are needed in **urban** or **suburban** areas, than in **rural** areas. New York City, which has a **population** of 8 million people, has more than 35,000 police officers. Police departments in rural communities often have fewer than 10 officers.

Police recruits have to pass physical fitness and other kinds of tests in order to become sworn officers.

Before any person becomes a police officer, they must go through training at a police academy. They learn about the laws of their region and the best way for police to respond to different situations. New recruits need training in using weapons and technology as well. They must respond with courage, authority, and respect to serve their communities.

Breach of Trust

Most police officers are honest, hard working protectors of the peace. Corrupt officers may willingly fail to fight crime, accept **bribes**, or commit acts of needless **brutality**. They are often judged harshly for betraying the public trust.

11

In large departments, different officers perform specific jobs, or **details**. It is a little bit like playing a position on a sports team. There are uniformed patrol officers out on the street, traffic and transit police, plain-clothes officers, criminal detectives, and even **undercover** officers.

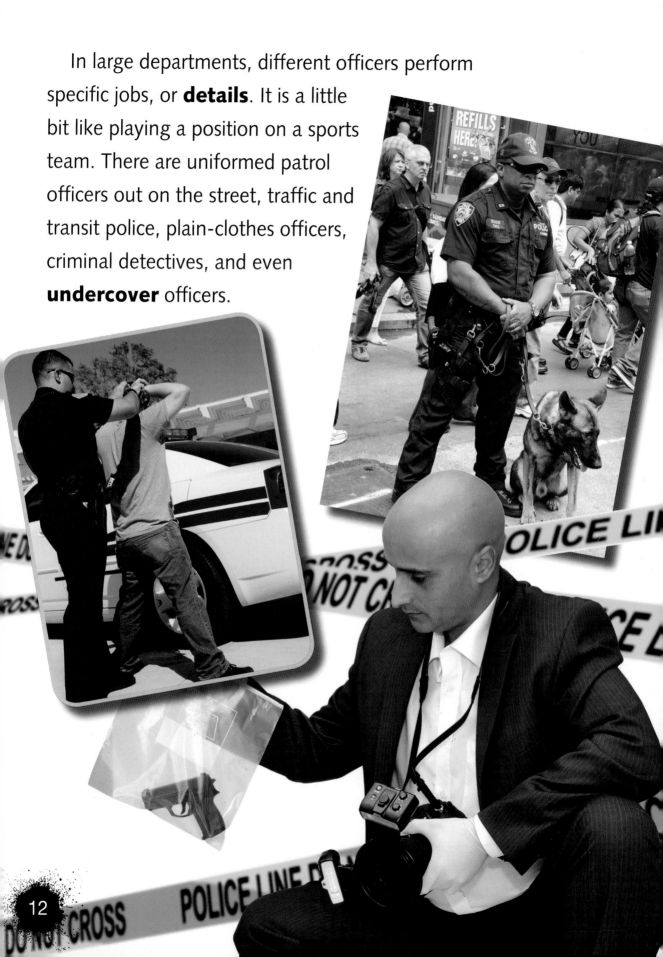

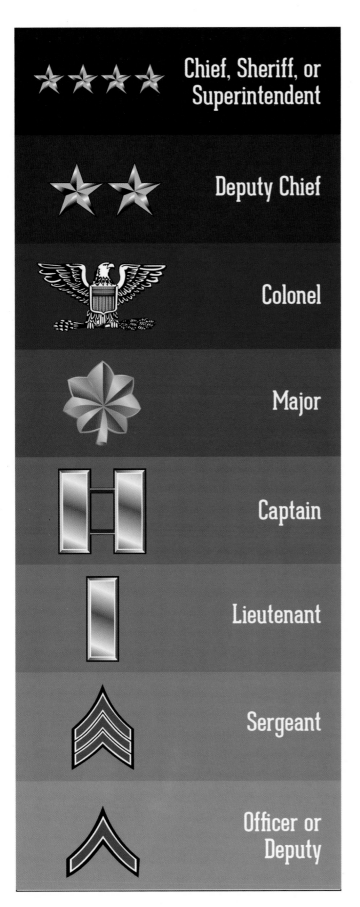

	Chief, Sheriff, or Superintendent
	Deputy Chief
	Colonel
	Major
	Captain
	Lieutenant
	Sergeant
	Officer or Deputy

Like the military, police use ranks to divide and manage their members. Most begin as officers. After years of service, an officer may take a test and apply for a promotion. Each rank has a different uniform, color, and emblem. Depending on the department, the highest rank is police chief, sheriff, or superintendent.

Police and Politics

In major U.S. cities the mayor usually **appoints** the police commander. A sheriff is an **elected** official, and is usually the highest ranking police officer in a particular county. The sheriff is responsible for overseeing the operation of the county jail.

The wide range of police duties helps big city departments keep the peace, respond to emergencies, investigate crimes, and make arrests. Police departments also take care of many other matters. Often, when there are hundreds of thousands, or even millions of people, living close together police are needed to keep events and other large gatherings safe and organized.

Some police departments in the United States and Canada use a strategy called community policing. The officers live in the community where they work and interact with the people. This helps to build trust and cooperation between the police and the public.

To save money, some urban departments have officers patrol neighborhoods on bicycles, rather than in squad cars.

In small towns, a single officer may have to perform many different police duties in the same day. Because people live further apart in rural areas, these officers may also have to travel several miles when responding to emergency calls.

Police work can be mysterious, suspenseful, and dramatic. Because of this, police work has become a popular source of entertainment in the U.S. and around the world.

Many popular books, TV shows, and movies feature the work of police officers, detectives, and the men and women of law enforcement.

While those shows are fun and entertaining, they are **fiction**. In reality, solving crimes often takes police much longer than a single hour. It typically takes months, years, or even decades of work. Keeping the peace and enforcing laws can be hard, grinding work. It is rewarding, but hardly glamorous.

Police and Guns

In the United States, police officers carry guns. TV shows and movies often portray police drawing or firing their guns at criminals. In real life, police rarely fire their weapons. When they do, it is a last resort in a life-threatening situation. Police in some countries, such as England, do not carry guns.

Regardless of where an officer works, certain tools are necessary to perform effective and safe police work. Items like handcuffs, a flashlight, and a radio are essential. For the officers' protection, they may also carry weapons.

A POLICE OFFICER'S DUTY BELT. Items worn on the belt usually include: handcuffs, service revolver (gun), pepper spray or mace, shock device (taser), night stick or expandable baton, flashlight, and a police radio.

shock device (taser)

Calling All Units

Police officers wear special two-way radios on their duty belts. These are like walkie-talkies that 9-1-1 dispatchers can use to alert them to trouble. When officers are notified of a robbery or other emergency taking place near them, they can quickly respond. Officers can also use them to call for help, or back-up.

As long as people have lived together in towns or cities, there has been a need for law and order. Throughout history, national armies or military groups often held responsibility for maintaining order, capturing criminals, and punishing offenders.

The first official paid police in the U.S. were the United States Marshals.

"Wild Bill" Hickok
(1837 – 1876)

President George Washington (1732-1799) appointed the first Marshals in 1789.

James Butler Hickok, known as "Wild Bill" Hickok, is one of the most famous U.S. Marshals.

20

The Marshals enforced rules handed down by the young nation's courts. They also protected judges and the president.

The modern idea of publicly financed police forces started 200 years ago in London, England. Soon cities around the world began adding police forces of their own.

Sir Robert Peel

(1788-1850)

Peelers: The First Modern Police

The first paid municipal police force formed in London, England in 1829. Named after their founder, British Prime Minister Sir Robert Peel, the Peelers kept the peace and enforced laws. Officially known as the Metropolitan Police, or Metropol, they reduced crime in London by working to prevent crimes rather than simply responding to them.

In addition to catching criminal suspects, police are often involved in dangerous rescue operations where people have been hurt. The police are the first ones called whenever there is danger.

From the first days of the U.S. Marshals and the British Peelers, up to present times, police officers deal with potentially deadly danger while on the job.

In 2013, more than 100 officers died in the line of duty across the United States.

Pooch Patrol

Many police departments use dogs to help them respond to emergencies and investigate crimes. Known as K-9 patrols, these dogs can help rescue injured people in a disaster. They also sniff out bomb materials, illegal drugs, and even materials used to start fires, in the case of arson investigations.

Computers in their squad cars help officers know if someone being pulled over for a traffic violation is also wanted for any other crimes.

While the world continues to change, so does the job of a police officer. Police must constantly adjust to new technologies that help them do their job. They must be trained to use new weapons and procedures. They must also stay up to date with any new laws. Most modern police forces now use computers in their squad cars.

DNA Evidence

DNA acts as a sort of unique fingerprint used to identify a suspect. Police detectives work with science labs in analyzing DNA taken from something as small as a human hair, chewing gum, food, or blood spilled at a crime scene. DNA evidence has not only helped catch criminals, but also helped wrongly accused suspects gain their freedom.

Police investigators who work at crime scenes now perform careful searches and collect trace evidence. They look for fibers, soil, fingerprints, and DNA evidence. Anything left behind may be helpful to police when tracking down the criminal.

25

More and more, police are using video **surveillance** networks to help them catch criminal activity as it happens.

Police in some cities like Chicago are also turning to scientific methods called **analytics** to scan data about the times and places where crimes happen. They use the data to predict where they should place officers to prevent crimes from happening.

Cameras can create controversy. Traffic cameras issuing tickets to drivers who did not break any laws have caused problems. Some cities have had to stop using the cameras to police traffic violations.

Many police departments have seen a drop in traditional crime like burglaries. Instead, they are dealing with a rise in technology crimes. Officers need to develop new methods to fight crimes like identity theft and cyber crimes. The detectives of the future will spend even more time investigating these kinds of crimes.

Whatever the emergency or crime, the men and women sworn to protect the communities they serve will remain poised to respond and keep the peace.

TIMELINE

1749:
Philadelphia creates first rudimentary police force in North America featuring wardens paid from a public tax.

1829:
Metropolitan Police established in London, England. The first professional modern municipal police force is founded.

1863:
Boston police begin carrying guns while on patrol.

1789:
President George Washington creates the U.S. Marshals. They are the first paid law enforcers in the U.S.

1838:
Following Metropol's lead, Boston forms the first paid police force in the U.S.

1888:
Metropol begins using bloodhounds to track scents as part of criminal investigations.

1893:
Marie Owen, a widow of a Chicago police officer, becomes the first woman employed by a police department.

1910:
Alice Stebbins Wells of the Los Angeles Police Department becomes the first female police officer.

1974:
Police begin using bulletproof vests.

1902:
Fingerprinting used as a method of identification.

1914:
First police cars are used.

2001:
More than 70 police officers are killed responding to the terrorist attacks in New York City and Washington, D.C. It remains the deadliest day in the history of U.S. law enforcement and first response.

GLOSSARY

analytics (an-uh-LIT-iks): scientific use of past data to predict future

appoints (uh-POINTS): assigning a title or job to someone

bribes (BRIBES): gifts given to someone so they won't report wrongdoing

brutality (broo-TAL-uh-tee): the use of unnecessary force or violence

capitol (KAP-uh-tuhl): the building that houses a state's government

details (DEE-tailz): specific patrols, like traffic, subways, or security

elected (i-LEKT-ed): chosen for an office by a vote

emergencies (i-MUR-juhn-seez): sudden, unexpected, dangerous situations

fiction (FIK-shuhn): stories that are made up

interstate (IN-tur-state): highway that connects multiple states

municipal (myoo-NISS-uh-puhl): to do with a town or city and its services

population (pop-yuh-LAY-shuhn): the number of people living in a certain place

rural (RUR-uhl): having to do with the countryside, as opposed to the city

society (suh-SYE-uh-tee): all people living in a country or area

suburban (suh-BUR-buhn): areas around the edge of a big city

sworn (SWORN): having taken an oath

taxes (TAK-sez): money paid by the public for basic services

undercover (UHN-der KUH-ver): in disguise, so as to blend in

urban (UR-buhn): having to do with cities, as opposed to the country

INDEX

SHOW WHAT YOU KNOW

1. When was the first paid police force established in the U.S.?
2. What are two things DNA evidence is used for?
3. What is fingerprinting used for?
4. When did police officers start using bulletproof vests?
5. Why have traffic cameras created such controversy?

WEBSITES TO VISIT

www.policek9.com
www.nleomf.org
www.discoverpolicing.org

About the Author

Tom Greve is a freelance writer from Chicago; a city served by the second largest police force in the U.S. He is married and has two children. He appreciates the work of all the good men and women of the police force, who work to maintain peace and justice.

Meet The Author!
www.meetREMauthors.com

www.rourkeeducationalmedia.com

PHOTO CREDITS: Cover© DavidPinoPhotography; Page 4 © Bevan Goldswain; Page 5 © TFoxFoto, Page 5a © bikeriderlondon; Page 6-7 © Lane V. Erickso; Page 8 © iofoto; Page 10-11 © Daryl Lang Page 11 © bikeriderlondon; Page 12 © Lissandra Melo, Luis Louro, mikeledra; Page 14 © Jim Parkin Page 15 © miker; Page 17 © bikeriderlondon; Page 18 © James Mattil, Stephen Coburn; Page 19 © Ella Sarkisyan; Page 22 © bikeriderlondon; Page 22-23 © spirit of america; Page 24 © Christopher Ziemnowicz; Page 25 © arfo; Page 25a © kilukilu; Page 25b © Corepics VOF; Page 26-27 © Martynova Anna; Page 26 © Graham Taylor; Page 27 © Glynnis Jones; Page 29 U.S. Federal Government/FEMA

Edited by: Jill Sherman

Designed and Produced by: Nicola Stratford   www.nicolastratford.com

Library of Congress Cataloging-in-Publication Data

Greve. Tom.
  Police: Protect and Serve / Tom Greve
  p. cm. -- (Emergency Response)
  ISBN 978-1-62717-653-8 (hard cover) (alk. paper)
  ISBN 978-1-62717-775-7 (soft cover)
  ISBN 978-1-62717-894-5 (e-book)
  Library of Congress Control Number: 2014934246

Rourke Educational Media
Printed in the United States of America,
North Mankato, Minnesota

Also Available as:

ROURKE'S
e-Books